FIRST REPERTOIRE FOR
FLUTE
with piano

edited, selected and arranged by
ausgewählt, herausgegeben und bearbeitet von
choisi, édité et arrangé par

Sally Adams
&
Nigel Morley

© 2003 by Faber Music Ltd
First published in 2003 by Faber Music Ltd
3 Queen Square London WC1N 3AU
Cover illustration by Drew Hillier
Cover design by Nick Flower
Music processed by Jackie Leigh
Printed in England by Caligraving Ltd

ISBN 0-571-52163-0

FABER *ff* MUSIC

CONTENTS

To buy Faber Music publications or to find out about the full range of titles available
please contact your local music retailer or Faber Music sales enquiries:

Faber Music Limited, Burnt Mill, Elizabeth Way, Harlow, CM20 2HX England
Tel: +44 (0)1279 82 89 82   Fax: +44 (0)1279 82 89 83
sales@fabermusic.com   fabermusic.com

Song without words

attributed Franz Paul Lachner
(1803–1890)

4

Walking in shadows

Pam Wedgwood

Fine

D.C. al Fine

Where, oh where do I live?

Harry Carlton

Minuet
from *Il Pastor Fido*

George Frideric Handel
(1685–1759)

Rocky's rodeo

Sally Adams

12

Walking in the air

from *The Snowman*

Howard Blake

Spagnoletta

Michael Praetorius
(1571–1621)

Long Lankin

Traditional
arranged Sally Adams

Coming from the fountain

Enrique Granados
(1867–1916)

Cortesemente
Third movement from Sonata in A

Georg Philipp Telemann
(1681–1767)

Grandmama tells a ghost story

Theodor Kullak
(1818–1882)

Tell them Martha sent you

Sarah Watts

Romance

Max Reger
(1873–1916)

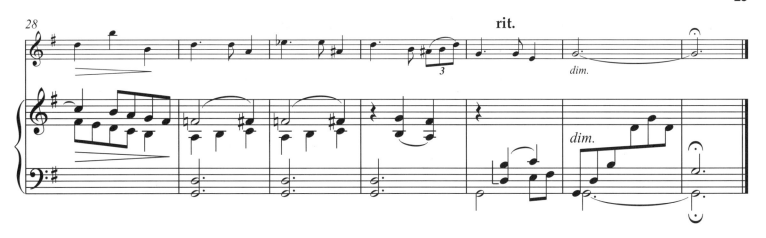

Andante alla Siciliana
2nd movement from Flute Concerto

Saverio Mercadante
(1795–1870)

The Vicar of Dibley

Howard Goodall

Tell me lovely shepherd

William Boyce
(1711–1779)

Andante sempre con moto piacevole (♩. = c.60)

Hungarian Fantaisie

Karl Joachim Andersen
(1847–1909)

Andante espressivo (♩ = c.72)